I0477816

Table of Contents

Introduction: The Exciting World of Juice Bar Entrepreneurship

Starting a juice bar business can be one of the most thrilling and rewarding ventures for those with a passion for health and wellness. Imagine providing your community with delicious, nutritious beverages that not only taste great but also promote a healthy lifestyle. This guide is here to walk you through the essential steps and considerations for launching and running a successful juice bar business.

Chapter 1: The Juice Bar Business and Its Benefits

First, let's dive into the concept of a juice bar business and its crucial role in promoting a healthy lifestyle. A juice bar isn't just a place to grab a refreshing drink; it's a hub for health-conscious individuals looking for nutritious options. Starting this type of business has numerous benefits, such as contributing to the growing demand for healthy beverages and creating a positive impact on your community's well-being. This chapter will give you an overview of the guide's purpose and structure, ensuring you have a clear roadmap for your journey.

Chapter 2: Assessing Your Skills and Resources

Before diving into the nuts and bolts of running a juice bar, it's essential to take a step back and assess your skills and resources. Do you have a background in health, nutrition, or the food and beverage industry? Are you passionate about providing healthy options to others? This chapter will help you evaluate your strengths and areas of expertise, as well as identify the resources available to you, such as finances, location, and equipment. Understanding these elements is key to maximizing your chances of success.

Chapter 3: Understanding Your Target Market

Knowing your target market is crucial for any business, and a juice bar is no exception. In this chapter, we'll guide you through the process of identifying and defining your target market segments. Whether your potential customers are health-conscious individuals, fitness enthusiasts, or busy professionals, understanding their preferences, dietary habits, and spending patterns will help you tailor your offerings. Conducting thorough market research will enable you to identify opportunities for differentiation and specialization, ensuring your juice bar stands out.

Chapter 4: Developing Your Menu and Recipes

A great juice bar menu offers a variety of fresh juices, smoothies, and healthy snacks that cater to diverse tastes. In this chapter, we'll delve into the art of designing a menu that attracts and retains customers. You'll learn how to source high-quality fruits, vegetables, and other ingredients, and create unique flavor combinations and signature drinks that appeal to your target audience. A well-crafted menu can give your juice bar a competitive edge and keep customers coming back for more.

Chapter 5: Setting Up Your Juice Bar

Location, location, location! Choosing the right spot for your juice bar is vital for attracting customers. In this chapter, we'll discuss factors to consider, such as foot traffic, visibility, and proximity to your target market. We'll also guide you through designing an inviting and functional space, including seating areas, menu boards, and decor. Finally, we'll cover selecting and installing the necessary equipment for juice preparation and storage, ensuring a smooth and efficient operation.

Chapter 6: Legal and Regulatory Considerations

Navigating the legal landscape is a crucial part of starting any business. This chapter will cover the permits, licenses, and health regulations specific to juice bar operations. We'll emphasize the importance of complying with food safety and hygiene standards to protect your customers' health and well-being. By implementing policies and procedures for ingredient sourcing, preparation, and storage, you can ensure your juice bar meets all health and safety guidelines.

Chapter 7: Marketing and Promotion Strategies

Raising awareness and attracting customers to your juice bar requires a comprehensive marketing plan. In this chapter, we'll explore various strategies, including social media, local advertising, and community events. You'll learn how to create brand awareness and drive traffic to your juice bar through promotions, loyalty programs, and special events. Effective marketing can significantly boost your business's visibility and customer base.

Chapter 8: Providing Exceptional Service

Customer service can make or break your juice bar. In this chapter, we'll focus on training your staff to offer friendly and knowledgeable service, including menu recommendations and nutritional information. Efficient order-taking, preparation, and delivery are essential to minimize wait times and enhance the overall customer experience. Creating a welcoming and positive atmosphere with clean and well-maintained facilities will ensure customer satisfaction and loyalty.

Chapter 9: Managing Operations and Finances

Running a successful juice bar requires effective management of operations and finances. This chapter will explore establishing efficient workflows for inventory management, order fulfillment, and cash handling. We'll also discuss monitoring expenses, revenue, and profitability to maintain financial stability. Implementing cost-saving measures and strategies to maximize profitability and minimize waste will help sustain your business in the long run.

Chapter 10: Growing Your Juice Bar Business

Once your juice bar is up and running, you'll want to think about growth. This chapter will discuss strategies for expanding your menu offerings, opening additional locations, or partnering with fitness centers or health-focused businesses. Community engagement through events, workshops, and collaborations can build brand loyalty and support local initiatives, helping your business thrive and reach new markets.

Throughout this guide, our goal is to provide you with a comprehensive and practical resource for starting and running a successful juice bar. By making informed decisions, tailoring your offerings to your target market, and providing exceptional service, you can create a thriving and profitable juice bar. So, let's dive in and explore the exciting world of juice bar entrepreneurship together!

Chapter 1: Introduction to the Juice Bar Business

Starting a juice bar business is a thrilling and rewarding venture for any entrepreneur. In our fast-paced world, where more and more people are placing a premium on their health and wellness, juice bars are booming in popularity. These establishments offer a variety of fresh and delicious beverages that are not only tasty but also packed with essential nutrients. In this chapter, we'll delve into the fundamentals of the juice bar business and explore the significant role it plays in providing healthy and refreshing beverage options.

Defining the Juice Bar Business

So, what exactly is a juice bar? In a nutshell, a juice bar is a place that specializes in serving a variety of freshly squeezed juices, smoothies, and other healthy beverages. These establishments are dedicated to providing customers with nutritious options that help them achieve their health and fitness goals. Juice bars usually offer a wide range of choices, catering to different tastes and dietary restrictions. Whether it's classic combinations like orange juice or green smoothies, or more unique blends that incorporate exotic fruits and vegetables, juice bars have something for everyone. The focus is always on using fresh, high-quality ingredients to ensure the best possible taste and nutritional value.

The Benefits of Starting a Juice Bar Business

There are many benefits to starting a juice bar business. First and foremost, you get the chance to contribute positively to the health and well-being of your community. By offering nutritious and delicious beverages, you can help people make healthier choices and improve their overall diet.

Additionally, the demand for healthy beverage options is on the rise. As more individuals become health-conscious, they are actively seeking alternatives to sugary sodas and artificial drinks. A juice bar business has the potential to attract a wide range of customers, including fitness enthusiasts, health-conscious individuals, and those looking for convenient meal replacements.

Moreover, starting a juice bar business allows you to tap into a growing market. With the increasing popularity of wellness trends and a focus on preventive healthcare, juice bars have become an essential part of many people's daily routines. By meeting this demand, you can build a loyal customer base and achieve long-term success.

The Purpose and Structure of This Guide

The purpose of this guide is to provide aspiring entrepreneurs with a comprehensive resource for starting and running a successful juice bar business. Each chapter will cover various aspects of the business, from assessing your skills and resources, understanding your target market, and developing your menu and recipes, to setting up your juice bar, navigating legal and regulatory considerations, implementing marketing strategies, and managing operations and finances.

By following this guide, you'll gain valuable insights, practical tips, and step-by-step instructions to help you navigate the process of starting and growing your juice bar business. Whether you're a seasoned entrepreneur or venturing into the food and beverage industry for the first time, this guide will equip you with the knowledge and tools you need to succeed.

Now, let's dive into the first step: assessing your skills and resources for the juice bar business. This is where your journey begins, and we'll make sure you have a solid foundation to build on. Ready? Let's get started!

Chapter 2: Assessing Your Skills and Resources

Starting a successful juice bar business is an exciting journey, but it all begins with understanding your own skills and the resources you have at your disposal. In this chapter, we'll dive deep into evaluating your background, experience, and passion for health and nutrition. We'll also help you identify your strengths and areas of expertise within the food and beverage industry. Plus, we'll explore the essential resources you'll need, including finances, location, and equipment.

Evaluating Your Background, Experience, and Passion

Before you jump into the world of juice bars, it's important to take a moment and reflect on your personal journey with health and wellness. Have you always been interested in leading a healthy lifestyle? Do you have any experience or knowledge in the food and beverage industry?

Think about your passion for health and nutrition. If you find yourself constantly reading about new health trends, experimenting with nutritious recipes, or advising friends on healthy choices, then you're already on the right path. Passion is a powerful motivator. When you genuinely care about health and nutrition, it shows. Your enthusiasm will shine through in your interactions with customers, making them more likely to return because they feel your dedication to providing high-quality, nutritious beverages.

Having a solid understanding of health and nutrition also gives you a significant advantage. It allows you to create menu items that cater to specific dietary needs and preferences, setting your juice bar apart from the competition.

Identifying Your Strengths and Expertise

Running a successful juice bar isn't just about making great drinks; it's also about leveraging your strengths and expertise. Take some time to think about your skills and knowledge in areas such as customer service, culinary expertise, marketing, or operations management.

Perhaps you have previous experience in the hospitality industry. This experience can be incredibly valuable, as it provides a deep understanding of customer service and team management. Maybe you have a background in nutrition or culinary arts, which allows you to develop unique and healthy recipes that will delight your customers.

Identifying your strengths will help you leverage your expertise and stand out in the competitive juice bar market. And don't forget about partnerships! Teaming up with a local fitness expert or a nutritionist can add tremendous value to your business and attract a broader range of customers. Collaborations like these can complement your skills and provide a richer experience for your customers.

Determining Your Resources

Starting a juice bar business also requires careful consideration of the resources available to you. These resources include finances, location, and equipment.

Finances

First, evaluate your financial situation. How much capital do you have to invest in your juice bar? Calculate your start-up costs, which will include rent, utility bills, equipment purchases, inventory, and initial marketing expenses. If you find that you need additional funding, explore options like small business loans, grants, or partnerships. Knowing your financial standing will help you make informed decisions and avoid potential pitfalls.

Location

Choosing the right location for your juice bar is crucial. Think about factors such as foot traffic, visibility, proximity to your target market, and accessibility. A great location can significantly impact your success. Make sure to research local zoning laws and regulations to ensure compliance before finalizing your location.

Equipment

Next, determine the equipment you'll need to operate your juice bar efficiently. This includes commercial-grade juicers, blenders, refrigeration units, storage containers, and serving equipment. Research reputable suppliers and compare prices to ensure you choose equipment that suits your needs and fits within your budget.

By thoroughly assessing your skills, expertise, and available resources, you will gain valuable insights into whether starting a juice bar business is the right path for you. This self-evaluation will also help you plan and strategize effectively, setting the foundation for a successful venture.

Embarking on this journey with a clear understanding of your strengths and resources will not only make the process smoother but also increase your chances of building a thriving juice bar that reflects your passion for health and nutrition.

Chapter 3: Understanding Your Target Market

Alright, let's dive into the heart of your business: your target market. Think of this as the group of people who are most likely to be interested in and excited about what you have to offer. In this chapter, we're going to explore how to define who these people are, how to conduct market research to really get to know them, and how to identify opportunities to make your juice bar stand out from the crowd.

Defining Your Target Market Segments

First things first, let's talk about defining your target market segments. These are specific groups of people who share similar characteristics and, more importantly, are likely to need or want your products. For a juice bar, your target market segments might look something like this:

- **Health-Conscious Individuals:** These are people who prioritize their physical well-being and are always on the lookout for nutritious and healthy food options.
- **Fitness Enthusiasts:** This group includes those who are regularly active and seek out products that can support their active lifestyles.

- **Busy Professionals:** Think of individuals who lead hectic lives and appreciate the convenience of quick yet nutritious food and beverage options.

When you're defining these segments, consider factors like age, gender, location, lifestyle preferences, and dietary restrictions. Understanding these specifics allows you to tailor your marketing efforts and menu offerings to better meet their needs.

Conducting Market Research

Once you've identified your target market segments, the next step is to conduct thorough market research. This is where you really get to know your potential customers—their preferences, dietary habits, and spending patterns. Here are some methods you can use:

- **Surveys and Questionnaires:** Create surveys to gather information about your target market's preferences, habits, and attitudes towards healthy beverages. You can distribute these surveys online or in person at places like gyms or health food stores.
- **Focus Groups:** Bring together a small group of individuals from your target market segments to have open discussions about their needs and preferences. This method can provide deep insights into what drives their purchasing decisions.
- **Competitor Analysis:** Take a close look at your competitors. Understand their target

market, menu offerings, pricing strategies, and marketing tactics. This analysis can help you identify opportunities to differentiate your juice bar and specialize in areas your competitors might be overlooking.

Identifying Opportunities for Differentiation and Specialization

Through your market research, you'll likely uncover opportunities to make your juice bar unique and better meet the needs of your target market. For instance, you might find that there's a demand for juice bars catering to specific dietary restrictions, like gluten-free or vegan options. By offering a diverse range of menu items that cater to these needs, you can attract a niche market and create a unique selling point for your business.

Another way to differentiate your juice bar could be by offering personalized juice options. Let customers choose their preferred fruits and vegetables to create a customized beverage. This personalization can enhance the customer experience, giving them a sense of ownership over their drink choices.

Additionally, you might identify a unique selling proposition by partnering with local organic farms or sustainable suppliers. Ensuring the highest quality and freshest ingredients can resonate with health-conscious consumers who prioritize sustainability. This commitment to ethical and environmentally friendly sourcing can set your juice bar apart.

By understanding your target market segments, conducting thorough market research, and identifying opportunities for differentiation and specialization, you'll be well-positioned to attract and retain loyal customers.

What's Next?

In the next chapter, we'll dive into the exciting process of developing your menu and recipes. We'll explore how to create a menu that not only attracts customers but also showcases your creativity and commitment to providing healthy, delicious options. Get ready to let your culinary imagination run wild!

Chapter 4: Developing Your Menu and Recipes

Welcome to the world of menu development for your juice bar! A well-crafted menu is essential not just for attracting customers, but also for showcasing your creativity, quality, and commitment to healthy, delicious options. Let's explore the key aspects of developing an enticing menu and crafting recipes that will leave your customers coming back for more.

Designing a Menu with a Variety of Fresh Juices, Smoothies, and Healthy Snacks

A successful juice bar menu should offer a wide selection of options to cater to the diverse tastes and preferences of your customers. This means providing a variety of fresh juices, smoothies, and healthy snacks that tantalize the taste buds while delivering essential nutrients.

Start by brainstorming a list of your favorite juice combinations and smoothie recipes. Think about incorporating popular ingredients like kale, spinach, ginger, berries, and tropical fruits. Experiment with different flavor profiles, textures, and garnishments to create a unique and exciting menu.

To make the menu easy to navigate, categorize your offerings into sections such as "Refreshing Juices," "Creamy Smoothies," and "Nutritious Snacks." Provide clear descriptions of each item, highlighting the ingredients, health benefits, and flavor profiles. This helps customers make informed choices and encourages them to try new and exciting options.

Sourcing High-Quality Fruits, Vegetables, and Other Ingredients

The key to creating exceptional juices and smoothies lies in using high-quality ingredients. Seek out local suppliers, farmers' markets, and organic farms that offer fresh, seasonal produce. By sourcing locally, you not only support the community but also ensure the freshness, flavor, and nutritional value of your ingredients.

Consider partnering with sustainable suppliers who prioritize eco-friendly and ethical practices. This can help build your reputation as a responsible and environmentally conscious juice bar, attracting customers who share similar values.

In addition to fruits and vegetables, explore unique ingredients and superfoods that can elevate your recipes. Ingredients like chia seeds, hemp hearts, turmeric, or spirulina are known for their health benefits and can add an interesting twist to your menu.

Creating Unique Flavor Combinations and Signature Drinks

Differentiating your juice bar from competitors is crucial, and one effective way to do this is by creating unique flavor combinations and signature drinks. Experiment with various flavor profiles to develop recipes exclusive to your juice bar. Consider incorporating local or regional flavors that resonate with your target audience.

For example, if your juice bar is located in a coastal area, you could create a signature drink using fresh coconut water or tropical fruits commonly found in the region. This helps create a sense of place and uniqueness that sets your juice bar apart.

Another way to create signature drinks is by partnering with local influencers, nutritionists, or fitness experts to develop recipes tailored to their expertise or brand. Collaborations like these not only provide you with innovative recipes but also help increase brand awareness and credibility.

Remember to include eye-catching names and descriptions for your signature drinks that capture the essence of the flavors and ingredients. This will pique customers' curiosity and make them more likely to try these specialty creations.

Wrapping It Up

In summary, developing an appealing and diverse menu is essential for any successful juice bar. By offering a wide range of fresh juices, smoothies, and healthy snacks, sourcing high-quality ingredients, and creating unique flavor combinations and signature drinks, you can create a menu that entices your target audience and keeps them coming back for more. So, let your creativity flow and create a menu that delights and nourishes your customers.

Chapter 5: Setting Up Your Juice Bar

Setting up your juice bar is an exciting and crucial phase of your business journey. It requires thoughtful consideration of several key factors, including choosing the right location, designing a welcoming space, and installing the necessary equipment. Let's dive into these steps in detail to ensure your juice bar is primed for success.

Choosing a Suitable Location

The location of your juice bar can significantly impact its success. You want a spot that's not only accessible but also highly visible to your target customers. Here are some important factors to keep in mind:

Foot Traffic

You should look for areas with high foot traffic, such as shopping centers, busy streets, or near gyms and fitness centers. These locations naturally attract more people, increasing the chances of potential customers stopping by your juice bar.

Visibility

Your juice bar needs to catch the eye of passersby. Opt for a location with good visibility, perhaps a spot with large windows where you can display colorful, eye-catching signage or decorations outside. This will help draw attention and entice people to come in and see what you have to offer.

Proximity to Target Market

Consider how close your juice bar is to your target market. If your ideal customers are health-conscious individuals or busy professionals, it makes sense to situate your juice bar near offices, yoga studios, or fitness centers. This way, you'll be conveniently located for those looking for a quick, healthy refreshment.

Designing an Inviting Space

The design of your juice bar plays a crucial role in attracting and keeping customers. You want to create an environment that feels inviting and functional. Here are some tips to help you design a space that customers will love:

Seating Areas

Provide comfortable seating areas where customers can relax and enjoy their drinks. Incorporate a mix of communal tables and individual seating options to cater to different preferences. Think about how you can create a cozy, social atmosphere that encourages customers to stay longer and perhaps order more.

Menu Boards

Make sure your menu is displayed clearly and prominently. Use menu boards that are easy to read and update. Digital menu boards can be a great option, as they allow for quick changes and add a modern touch to your juice bar.

Decor

Your decor should reflect a fresh and energetic vibe that aligns with your brand image. Use natural elements like plants, wooden accents, and vibrant artwork to create a welcoming atmosphere. The right decor can make your juice bar a place where customers feel happy and eager to return.

Installing Equipment

Having the right equipment is essential for the smooth operation of your juice bar. Here's a rundown of the key items you'll need:

Commercial Juicers and Blenders

Invest in high-quality commercial juicers and blenders. These machines should be capable of efficiently and effectively preparing a wide range of juices and smoothies. Consider their capacity and speed to ensure they can handle the demands of your busy juice bar.

Refrigeration Units

Install reliable refrigeration units to store and preserve fresh fruits, vegetables, and other perishable ingredients. Proper refrigeration is crucial for maintaining the quality and safety of your products.

Other Equipment

Don't forget the smaller, yet equally important, pieces of equipment. This includes cutting boards, knives, measuring cups, and storage containers. These tools are essential for the daily operations of your juice bar, helping you prepare and serve your beverages efficiently.

By carefully selecting a suitable location, designing an inviting space, and installing the necessary equipment, you'll create a juice bar that not only attracts customers but also provides a delightful and memorable experience. In the next chapter, we'll explore the legal and regulatory considerations you need to be aware of when starting a juice bar business. Stay tuned!

Chapter 6: Legal and Regulatory Considerations

Starting a juice bar business is a thrilling adventure, but it also comes with a significant responsibility to understand and adhere to various legal requirements and regulations. To run a successful and compliant operation, it's essential to familiarize yourself with the necessary permits, licenses, and health regulations. Additionally, you must comply with regulations governing food safety, hygiene standards, and sanitation practices. This chapter will guide you through the key considerations when it comes to the legal and regulatory aspects of running a juice bar business.

Understanding Legal Requirements

Before you can open the doors of your juice bar, it's crucial to understand the legal requirements specific to your location. This involves obtaining the necessary permits and licenses from local, state, and federal authorities. These may include:

- A business license
- A food establishment permit
- A health department permit
- Any other permits or licenses that are applicable in your area

The first step is to research and reach out to your local health department or regulatory agencies.

They will provide you with the specific requirements and documentation needed to open a juice bar. This initial research is vital to ensure you comply with all relevant laws and avoid any legal issues down the road.

Food Safety and Hygiene Standards

Food safety is paramount when running a juice bar. Ensuring your customers receive safe, high-quality products is crucial for both your reputation and your success. Complying with food safety and hygiene standards will help you maintain a clean and sanitary environment for both preparation and service.

Implementing proper policies and procedures for ingredient sourcing, preparation, and storage is vital to prevent contamination and maintain product integrity. This includes regularly inspecting and monitoring the quality and freshness of fruits, vegetables, and other ingredients. Additionally, establish guidelines for proper handling, washing, and cutting of produce to avoid cross-contamination.

Maintaining proper hygiene practices is equally important. Ensure that your staff members wear clean and appropriate clothing, practice proper hand hygiene, and follow all sanitation procedures. Regular cleaning and sanitization of equipment, utensils, and surfaces should be enforced to prevent the growth of bacteria and other harmful microorganisms.

Ingredient Sourcing and Storage

To ensure compliance with health and safety guidelines, it's essential to establish policies and procedures for ingredient sourcing and storage. This includes working with reputable suppliers who adhere to strict quality control measures and provide fresh, high-quality produce. When selecting suppliers, consider factors such as their reputation, certifications, and commitment to sustainable and ethical sourcing practices.

Regularly inspect and monitor incoming ingredients to ensure they meet your quality standards. Proper storage practices are vital to maintaining the freshness and safety of your ingredients. Implement systems for proper refrigeration and storage temperature control to prevent spoilage and reduce the risk of foodborne illnesses. Additionally, establish procedures for labeling and dating ingredients to ensure proper rotation and minimize waste.

By understanding and complying with legal requirements and regulations, as well as implementing robust food safety practices, you can create a safe and compliant environment for your juice bar business. This will not only protect the health and well-being of your customers but also contribute to the long-term success of your business.

Running a juice bar involves much more than just serving delicious and nutritious drinks. It requires a deep understanding of the legal landscape and a commitment to maintaining the highest standards of food safety and hygiene. By doing so, you'll build a strong foundation for your business and ensure its growth and prosperity in the competitive world of health-focused dining.

Now that we've covered the legal and regulatory considerations, you're one step closer to making your juice bar dream a reality. Next, we'll explore how to develop a mouthwatering menu that will keep your customers coming back for more. Let's get started!

Chapter 7: Marketing and Promotion Strategies

To make your juice bar a buzzing success, you need a rock-solid marketing and promotion plan. This chapter will walk you through developing effective strategies to raise awareness and attract customers to your juice bar, ensuring your business thrives in a competitive market.

Developing a Marketing Plan

The first step on your marketing journey is to craft a comprehensive marketing plan. This plan will be your roadmap, outlining your goals and objectives and detailing the strategies and tactics you'll use to achieve them. Let's break it down into key elements:

Identify Your Target Audience

Before you can effectively market your juice bar, you need to know who you're marketing to. Identify and understand your target audience by defining their demographic and psychographic profiles. What are their preferences and habits when it comes to consuming healthy beverages? Are they fitness enthusiasts, busy professionals, or health-conscious parents? Understanding your audience will help you tailor your marketing efforts to meet their needs and preferences.

Set Clear Goals and Objectives

What do you hope to achieve through your marketing efforts? Do you want to increase brand awareness, attract new customers, or encourage repeat visits? Setting specific and measurable goals that align with your overall business objectives is crucial. For instance, your goal might be to increase your social media following by 20% in three months or to boost in-store sales by 15% over the next quarter.

Utilize Online Marketing Channels

In today's digital age, having a strong online presence is essential. Leverage social media platforms like Facebook, Instagram, and Twitter to engage with your target audience, share updates and promotions, and showcase your menu offerings. Post high-quality, visually appealing content consistently to attract and retain followers. Share behind-the-scenes glimpses of your juice bar, highlight customer testimonials, and run interactive campaigns to keep your audience engaged.

Leverage Local Advertising

While online marketing is crucial, don't overlook traditional local advertising channels. Advertise in newspapers, on the radio, and in local magazines that your target audience reads. Collaborate with other local businesses to cross-promote each other. For example, a nearby gym could distribute flyers for your juice bar, while you could offer their members a discount on their first purchase.

Participate in Community Events

Getting involved in community events is a fantastic way to raise awareness and build relationships with potential customers. Sponsor or participate in health and fitness fairs, farmers' markets, or local fundraisers. Offer free samples of your juices and share information about the benefits of consuming fresh and healthy beverages. These events provide an excellent opportunity to connect with your community and create a positive impression of your brand.

Offering Promotions and Loyalty Programs

Promotions and loyalty programs are effective strategies to incentivize repeat visits and encourage customer referrals. Here are some ideas to consider:

Create Special Promotions

Offer limited-time promotions or discounts to attract new customers. For example, you could have a "buy one, get one free" promotion on select juices during specific hours or days. This not only encourages trial but also increases the likelihood of customers returning in the future. Promote these special offers through your social media channels, email newsletters, and in-store signage.

Implement a Loyalty Program

Reward your customers for their loyalty by implementing a loyalty program. This could be a points-based system where customers earn points for every purchase and can redeem them for discounts or free items. Promote your loyalty program through signage in your store, on your website, and via your social media channels. Make it easy for customers to join and track their points to keep them coming back.

Encourage Customer Referrals

Word-of-mouth marketing is incredibly powerful. Encourage your satisfied customers to refer their friends and family to your juice bar by offering incentives, such as a free juice or a discount on their next purchase. Provide referral cards that customers can give to their friends, or implement a referral program through your website or social media channels. The more your existing customers spread the word, the more new customers you'll attract.

By developing a solid marketing plan and implementing effective promotional strategies, you can raise awareness and attract customers to your juice bar. Remember to stay consistent with your messaging and engage with your audience through various online and offline channels. With a thoughtful approach and a bit of creativity, your marketing efforts will help your juice bar stand out and succeed.

Chapter 8: Providing Exceptional Service and Experience

Creating a fantastic customer experience is the cornerstone of a successful juice bar business. Your goal is to ensure that every visit to your juice bar leaves a lasting, positive impression. In this chapter, we will explore various strategies and best practices to deliver top-notch customer service and maintain a delightful atmosphere in your juice bar.

Train Your Staff

Let's start with your team. One of the most critical aspects of providing exceptional service is having a well-trained, knowledgeable, and enthusiastic staff. Your employees should not only be friendly and approachable but also well-informed about your menu and the benefits of your offerings.

Begin by offering comprehensive training on your menu. This includes the different types of juices, smoothies, and healthy snacks you serve. Make sure your team understands the nutritional benefits of each item, so they can confidently share this information with customers. This knowledge is particularly important when assisting customers with dietary restrictions and allergies. Your staff should know the ingredients in each recipe to provide accurate information and ensure customer safety.

Encourage continuous learning and development. Staying updated with the latest health trends and industry knowledge will allow your staff to better assist customers with their specific needs and preferences. This not only improves customer satisfaction but also shows that your juice bar is committed to offering the best possible service.

Efficient Order-Taking, Preparation, and Delivery

Efficiency is key in a juice bar, where customers expect quick and seamless service. To minimize wait times and enhance the overall customer experience, consider implementing these strategies:

1. **Streamline Your Ordering Process:** Invest in a user-friendly point-of-sale system that allows staff to take orders quickly and accurately. This reduces errors and speeds up the order-taking process.
2. **Optimize Your Production Workflow:** Arrange your equipment and workspaces to maximize efficiency. Train your staff on best practices for juice and smoothie preparation, emphasizing speed and accuracy. This setup can significantly reduce preparation time and improve service speed.
3. **Efficiently Manage Ingredient Inventory:** Keep a close eye on your ingredient inventory to ensure you always have a fresh supply of fruits, vegetables, and other necessary items. Regular monitoring helps avoid delays in preparation

and ensures you can fulfill customer orders promptly.

4. **Prioritize Cleanliness:** Maintain a clean and organized workspace, both in the front and back of the house. Regularly sanitize equipment, utensils, and prep surfaces to prevent cross-contamination and maintain food safety standards. Cleanliness not only ensures safety but also leaves a positive impression on customers.

Create a Welcoming Atmosphere

The atmosphere of your juice bar plays a significant role in shaping the customer experience. A welcoming and positive environment can turn a casual visit into a memorable experience. Here are some tips to create an inviting atmosphere:

1. **Comfortable Seating and Aesthetics:** Provide comfortable seating options where customers can relax and enjoy their drinks and snacks. Cozy chairs, booths, or even outdoor seating can enhance the customer experience. Pay attention to the aesthetics of your juice bar, using appealing decor and lighting to create a warm and inviting ambiance.
2. **Clean and Well-Maintained Facilities:** Regularly clean and maintain all areas of your juice bar, including restrooms, dining areas, and prep areas. A clean environment reassures customers about the quality and safety of your establishment.
3. **Personalized Interactions:** Train your staff to engage in friendly and personalized

interactions with customers. Encourage them to greet customers with a warm smile, learn and remember their names, and make them feel valued and appreciated. Personalized service can significantly enhance customer loyalty.

4. **Music and Ambiance:** Choose background music that complements the atmosphere of your juice bar. Soft, uplifting tunes can set a positive mood and enhance the overall customer experience.

Conclusion

By training your staff to provide exceptional service, optimizing your order-taking and preparation processes, and creating a welcoming atmosphere, you can ensure that your customers have a memorable experience each time they visit your juice bar. This not only boosts customer satisfaction but also encourages repeat business and positive word-of-mouth referrals. Every detail, from the friendliness of your staff to the cleanliness of your establishment, contributes to creating a space where customers love to spend time and enjoy healthy, delicious drinks.

Chapter 9: Managing Operations and Finances

Running a successful juice bar isn't just about serving up delicious, healthy drinks. It's also about efficiently managing your operations and finances to ensure long-term success. In this chapter, we'll dive into strategies for establishing efficient workflows, monitoring expenses and revenue, and implementing cost-saving measures to maximize profitability and minimize waste.

Establishing Efficient Workflows and Operational Procedures

To keep your juice bar running smoothly and maximize productivity, it's crucial to establish efficient workflows and operational procedures. Let's break down some key areas to focus on:

Inventory Management

Managing your inventory properly is essential to avoid wastage, ensure a consistent supply, and prevent stockouts. Develop a system to track inventory levels regularly and establish reorder points so you can replenish supplies in a timely manner. Using inventory management software can help streamline this process, making it easier to keep track of what you have and what you need.

Order Fulfillment

Clear and organized processes for taking and fulfilling customer orders are vital. Train your staff on efficient order-taking, preparation, and delivery methods. Utilizing technology, such as a user-friendly point-of-sale system, can help streamline the ordering process and minimize errors. This will lead to faster service and happier customers.

Cash Handling

Proper cash handling procedures are important to prevent errors and fraud. Train your staff on accurate cash handling practices, including counting cash, making change, and reconciling cash registers. Regularly performing cash audits can help ensure accuracy and catch any discrepancies early.

Monitoring and Tracking Expenses, Revenue, and Profitability

Maintaining financial stability and sustainability requires diligent monitoring and tracking of expenses, revenue, and profitability. Here are some important steps to consider:

Expense Tracking

Implement a system to track all expenses related to your juice bar business. This includes costs for ingredients, packaging, equipment maintenance, rent, utilities, and employee wages. By closely monitoring expenses, you can identify areas where costs can be reduced or optimized. Knowing exactly where your money is going helps you make informed decisions about your spending.

Revenue Tracking

Keep a detailed record of all sales and revenue generated by your juice bar. This will help you identify trends, measure the success of marketing initiatives, and make data-driven decisions to increase profitability. Understanding your revenue patterns can also help you forecast future sales and plan accordingly.

Profitability Analysis

Regularly analyze your business's profitability by comparing revenue and expenses. This will help you identify areas where you can improve margins, reduce costs, and increase overall profitability. Conducting these analyses periodically allows you to make adjustments and stay on top of your financial health.

Implementing Cost-Saving Measures and Strategies

Maximizing profitability and minimizing waste requires the implementation of effective cost-saving measures and strategies. Here are some approaches to consider:

Streamline Operational Processes

Continuously review and optimize your operational processes to eliminate inefficiencies, reduce waste, and minimize costs. Look for areas where workflow can be improved, such as ingredient preparation, juice production, and cleaning procedures. Small changes in these areas can lead to significant cost savings over time.

Control Ingredient Costs

Properly manage your ingredient inventory to minimize waste and control costs. Purchase ingredients in bulk to benefit from cost savings and negotiate favorable contracts with suppliers. Consider partnering with local farms or growers to source fresh ingredients directly, which can reduce transportation costs and support local businesses.

Minimize Energy Consumption

Implement energy-efficient practices to reduce utility costs. This includes using energy-efficient appliances, turning off lights and equipment when not in use, and optimizing temperature control. These small steps can add up to substantial savings on your utility bills.

Staff Training and Development

Investing in training and development programs for your staff can enhance their skills and productivity. Well-trained employees are more efficient in their roles, reducing errors and maximizing output. Providing ongoing training opportunities can also boost employee morale and retention, further benefiting your business.

By implementing these cost-saving measures and closely monitoring your expenses and revenue, you can ensure the financial stability and long-term success of your juice bar business. In the next chapter, we'll explore strategies for growing your juice bar business and expanding your customer base. Stay tuned for exciting insights on how to take your juice bar to the next level!

Chapter 10: Growing Your Juice Bar Business

Expanding Your Menu Offerings

To keep your juice bar buzzing with excitement and loyal customers, it's essential to regularly update and expand your menu offerings. As trends and customer preferences evolve, introducing new products or seasonal specials can keep your menu fresh and appealing. Think about experimenting with different flavor combinations and ingredients to create unique and delicious drinks that will make your customers eager to return.

Listening to customer feedback is crucial. Pay attention to popular trends in the industry and consider adding new types of juices, smoothies, or healthy snacks that align with your target market's preferences and needs. Customizable options can be a big hit too—let customers choose their own ingredients or add-ons for a more personalized experience. By continuously innovating and refreshing your menu, you'll attract new customers and keep your regulars engaged and excited about visiting your juice bar.

Expanding Your Reach

If you want to grow your customer base, it might be time to consider opening additional locations or partnering with other businesses in the health and wellness industry. Opening new locations is a significant step toward expanding your juice bar business. Look for areas with high foot traffic and a target market similar to your current location. Conduct thorough market research to ensure there's demand for your products in the new area. Consider factors like population demographics, local competition, and accessibility when selecting a new location.

Partnering with fitness centers, yoga studios, or other health-focused businesses can also be a strategic move. Collaborating with like-minded businesses opens up opportunities for cross-promotion and allows you to tap into an existing customer base that is likely interested in healthy and nutritious options. When considering partnerships, look for businesses that share similar values and target markets. Explore opportunities for joint events, workshops, or even co-branded products. By leveraging the existing customer base of your partners, you can reach a wider audience and increase brand exposure.

Engaging with Your Community

Building brand loyalty and supporting local initiatives are key aspects of growing your juice bar business. Engaging with your community through events, workshops, and collaborations can help you achieve these goals. Host events such as juice tastings, nutrition workshops, or cooking classes to create a sense of community and provide value beyond just selling products. These events not only showcase your expertise but also allow customers to experience your products in a more interactive and educational way.

Collaborating with local organizations, charities, or influencers can support community initiatives and demonstrate your commitment to improving the well-being of those around you. This could include partnering with a local farm to source fresh produce, sponsoring a community health fair, or donating a portion of your profits to a relevant cause. By actively participating in your community, you show your dedication to making a positive impact, which can help build strong brand loyalty.

In Conclusion

Growing your juice bar business requires continuous innovation and expansion. By expanding your menu offerings, opening additional locations, partnering with other businesses, and engaging with your community, you can attract new customers, retain existing ones, and establish a strong presence in the market. Remember to constantly listen to your customers, adapt to their changing preferences, and stay connected to the community you serve. Your dedication to these principles will pave the way for long-term success and a thriving juice bar business.